# Old Dogs' Wisdom

# Old Dogs' Wisdom

## Wise Words from Furry Friends

### Fiona Tomlinson

NEW HOLLAND

BELLA, 14, German Shepherd

To the dogs of the world who will never experience the wisdom of age or the the love of a human.

# WISDOM:

the quality of having experience, knowledge, and good judgement; the quality of being wise.

VULCAN, 14, Rotweiller x Mastiff

NINA, 9 Spinoni

# Introduction

I've spent most of my photographic career shooting people for magazines, for corporate portraiture and for TV, but my passion has always been photographing dogs and people with their dogs. You can tell a lot about a person by the way they talk about and interact with their animals and, in my opinion, the human/dog relationship is the ultimate leveller of all humans.

When I sent out my first casting call for older dogs on Facebook a few years ago I was overwhelmed with the response from people around the country. We are an enthusiastic lot us "dog-folk" when it comes to our canine friends and older dogs definitely seem to hold a very special place in our hearts.

I am grateful that my love affair with my first Giant Schnauzer Pola ignited my love for old dogs and prompted this collection of images. Pola wasn't my first dog, I grew up in a house full of dogs and all of them reached a grand old age, living out their lives in the sunniest and warmest parts of the house, but it was Pola who completely stole my heart from the minute she arrived aged eight weeks and inevitably broke it when she passed away aged 14 years.

She arrived a few weeks after my son Rogan was born. They grew up together, he learnt to walk hanging on to her and I lost my baby weight walking her. She was like my shadow and when she died I felt like I had lost a part of me. I had woken up to those black eyes each and every day and even though I could see her muzzle turning grey and her body slowing down, nothing much really changed. She still enjoyed swimming, running on the farm and above all – food!

This quality is really one of the most beautiful things about older dogs. It isn't their greying muzzles and eyebrows, although this is indeed a thing of great physical beauty, but it is their ability to enjoy each day as they did as a young dog. They might not chase that ball for the hours like they used to but they still like to chase that ball.

LENNON, 14, Staffordshire Terrier

PING, 12, Pekingese

# You can't help getting older, but you don't have to get old.

GEORGE BURNS

BILLY, 12, Hunterway X

ARABELLA, 11, Staffy x Mastiff

BANANAS, 12, Chihuahua X

BEAR, 11, German Shepherd

BARTY, 13, Mixed Breed

CROMWELL

ASH, 9, Husky

You think dogs will not be in heaven? I tell you, they will be there l o n g before any of us.

ROBERT LOUIS STEVENSON

BETTY, 13, Boxer

BESS, 15, German Shorthaired Pointer

BAXTER, 12, Golden Retreiver X

ANNIE, 13.5, English Bull Terrier

If there are no dogs in *heaven,* then when I die I want to go where *they* went.

WILL ROGERS

ARCHIE, 15, Jack Russell

BESS, 13, Staffordshire Terrier

BINTY, 9, Greyhound

BONNIE, 15, Labrador X

BREEZE, 13, Weimaraner

BIFFY, 12, Collie X

**Do not** go where the path may lead, go instead where there is no path and **leave a trail.**

RALPH WALDO EMERSON

BLAKE, 14, Brown Labrador

BRUCE, 8, Great Dane

ROGUE, 9, English Bull Terrier

RUBY, 9, Pug

# Be brave no matter your size.

BOB, 11, Dachshund

CHOPPA, 9, Bulldog x Boxer

RUBY, 12, Jack Russell X

SALV, 8, Saluki

CARA, 9. German Shepherd

# Don't accept your dog's *admiration* as conclusive <u>evidence</u> that you are *wonderful.*

ANN LANDERS

CASPER, 9, Chinese Crested

CHEVY, 10, Rotweiller

CLIFFORD, 8, COSTLEY, 11, CISSIE, 8, CRYSTAL, 12, Cavs

CHOPPER, 14, Dalmatian

# Let sleeping dogs lie.

SIR ROBERT WALPOLE

BUSTER, 12, Boxer x Staffy

CODY, 13, English Springer Spaniel

COCO, 12, German Shorthaired Pointer

RUSS, 12, Jack Russell X

RUBY, 16, Kelpie

# Sniff out opportunity.

BRACKEN, 10, Border Terrier

HENRY, 10, Corgi

DEVIL, 9.5, Shetland Sheepdog

COCO, 9, French Bull Dog

**Whatever you may look like, marry a man your own age – as your beauty *fades*, so will his *eyesight.***

PHYLLIS DILLER

CHARLIE, 10, Cavalier King Charles Spaniel

CHARLIE, 13, Tibetan Spaniel

BODIE, 12, Border Terrier

# Explore new paths.

BUDDY, 13, Belgium Shepherd X

DIGBY, 14, Hunterway x Border Collie

AVA, 11, Bitsa

DIXIE, 11.5, Standard Parti Poodle

# Age is an issue of mind over matter.
# If you don't mind, it doesn't matter.

MARK TWAIN

DUSTY, 11, Bitsa

DAISY LOUISE, 23, Terrier X

DUKE, 10, Pappillon x Chihuahua

DUKE, 14, Labrador

DUNHILL, 14, Jack Russell

Give *sloppy* wet nose kisses.

CHOPPER, 7, Staffy X

DYLAN, 10, Welsh Springer Spaniel

FRODO, 14, Kelpie

EMMA, 15, Golden Retriever

EMILY, 11, Tibetan Terrier

FROG, 15, Griffon

# It's not the size of the dog in the fight, it's the size of *fight* in the dog.

MARK TWAIN

STANLEY, 12, Bassett Hound X

SAM, 13, Collie x Hunterway

# Just remember, once you're over the **hill** you begin to pick up *speed*.

ARTHUR SCHOPENHAUER

ELLIE, 14, Labrador

GRACE, 12, Golden Retriever x Red Setter.

GYPSY, 12, Wire Haired Fox Terrier

INDI, 10, EVA, 12, German Shorthaired Pointers

HONEY, 13, Golden Retriever

# Nature *gives* you the face you have at twenty; it is up to you to *merit* the face you have at fifty.

COCO CHANEL

INDIE, 7, Great Dane

HOLLY, 14, Boxer

BILLY, 12, SAM, 13

ISIS, 11, Chihuahua

JACK, 12, Border Collie

# The world would be a *nicer* place if *everyone* had the ability to *love* as unconditionally as a dog.

M.K. CLINTON

JASMINE, 9, Staffordshire Bull Terrier

JACK, 13, Jack Russell

KODA, 10, Malamute

JACKY, 20, Shar Pei X

JACKY, 20, Star Pei X, JIFFY, 14, Westie & J.B, 15, Mixed Breed

SAMMIE, 9, Bernese Mountain Dog

# Be happy with what you have.

JESS, 10, Pomeranium x Papillon

JESS, 10, Golden Retriever X

JET, 14, Hunterway

JIFFY, 14, West Highland White Terrier

# If it wasn't for *dogs*, some people would <u>never</u> go for a *walk*.

KOBY, 14, Jack Russell

KHAN, 10, Staffy

KISSY, 9, Shetland Sheepdog

LADY, 13, Bitsa

LUCI, 14, Golden Retriever

HAVOC, 14, Kelpie X and RUSTY, 14, Jack Russell

# Be a best friend.

SAMMY, 8, Bullmastiff

LUCY, 17, Foxy X

LULU, 12, Rottweiler

LILLY, 13, Greyhound

# Never stop making your own FUN.

COCO, 12, Pomeranium x Chihuahua

MADDISON, 12.5, Labrador x Hunterway

MAJOR. 8. Rotweiller

MAISIE, 12, Golden Retriever

MATT, 10, Beagle

JACK BLACK, 10, Labrador

# It's not what you *look* at that matters, it's what you <u>see</u>.

HENRY DAVID THOREAU

MAXINE, 12, English Staffy

MEG, 12, Scottie

MERYL, 12, DENNY, 12, EVA, 12, German Shorthaired Pointer

JASMINE, 11, Pug

# Wrinkles should merely indicate where the smiles have been.

MARK TWAIN

MOJO, 12, Rhodesian Ridgeback X

MEG, 14, Hunterway X

MOLLY, 13, Black Labrador

MINNIE, 10.5, Chihuahua

To me – **old age**
is always
**ten years older**
than I am.

BERNARD BARUCH

MAC, 15, Foxy x Jack Russell

MILLIE, 10, Border Collie

MOLLY, 10, Mastiff X Great Dane

MONTY, 10, Shitzu

MOMO, 13, Staffy

JIP, 9, British Bulldog x Staffy

# Learn *new* tricks.

MOSES, 14, Staffy

JESUS, 12, Rhodesian Ridgeback X

# I don't need *you* to remind me of my *age*. I have a bladder to do that <u>for me.</u>

STEPHEN FRY

MAISEY, 15, Golden Retriever

MOSS, 12, Border Collie X

NUGGET, 14, Labrador

MAGGIE, 13, Jack Russell

# Honesty is the first chapter in the book of WISDOM.

THOMAS JEFFERSON

OPRAH, 14, Mini Poodle

OSCAR, 10, Teacup Maltese

OSWALD, 14, Griffon

PEPPER, 13, Giant Schnauzer

MEG, 14, Beardie X

The secret of staying young is to live honestly, eat slowly and **lie about your age.**

LUCILLE BALL

PENNY, 12, Labrador

PEPPER, 12, Dalamatian, ZAC, 8 Jack Russell

PIKACHU, 14, Dachshund

PEPPER, 17, Mixed Breed Terrier

MAX, 11, Wire Haired Jack Russell

# Dig life & chase your dreams.

PHOEBE, 14, Beagle

PHOENIX, 11, Malamute

MAX, 11, Wire Haired Jack Russell

PIPER, 12, Boxer

SAMSON, 8, Golden Retriever

# Dogs' lives are too short. Their *only* fault, really.

AGNES SLIGH TURNBULL

XENA, 14, Hunterway X

PUNGO, 14, Labroador x Staffy

KEITH, 10, Hunterway X

RIDDLES, 14, Hunterway X

# Let Hercules himself do what he may, The cat will mew and dog will have his day.

WILLIAM SHAKESPEARE, HAMLET

SAMSON, 8, Golden Retriever

ROCKY, 12, Shetland Sheepdog

SAMSON, 11, Doberman

SCRUFFY, 13, Bitsa

SHADOW, 12, Flat Coated Retriever

SPROCKET, 12. Belgium Shepherd

The reason a dog has so many friends; he *wags* his **tail** instead of his **tongue**.

AEROSMITH

SHARN, 12, Labrador X

SHEBA, 15.5, Crossbreed

NIBS, 13, Collie X

# Youth has *no age.*

PABLO PICASSO

SARAH, SHELBY, BRAMBLE, 9, Flat Coated Retrievers

SKYE, 14, Border Collie

# There are three faithful friends: an old wife, an old dog & ready money.

BENJAMIN FRANKLIN

My goal in life is to be as *good* of a person my dog already *thinks* I am.

SMIDGE, 10, Bitsa

SOUL, 11, Taiwanese Mountain Dog Cross

SPEAR, 15, Mixed Breed

KOGEE, 13, Mixed Breed

# Once you have had a *wonderful* dog, a life without one, is a life *diminished.*

DEAN KOONTZ

STEFFI, 14, Staffy

STEIN, 15, German Shorthaired Pointer

TESS, 10, German Shepherd

In life the *firmest* friend,
The **first** to welcome,
<u>foremost</u> to defend,
Whose honest heart is
still his master's own,
Who labours, fights, lives,
breathes for him **alone**.

LORD BYRON

STELLA, 13, Jack Russell

TAYZER, 9, Bullmastiff x Pitbull

BOSSKI, 14, Staffy

STELLA, 13, Pug

NEXUS, 7, Saint Bernard

# Take a
# NAP.

TOBY, 12, Irish Setter

TOBY, 9, Weimeraner

A boy can learn **a lot** from a dog: obedience, loyalty, and the importance of *turning* around **three** times **before** lying down.

ROBERT BENCHLEY

TOBY, 12, Wire Haired Jack Russell

TRIS, 16, Spinoni

SKIPPY, 10, Spitz X

SYDNEY, 14, Black Labrador

# The fool doth *think* he is wise, but the *wise* man knows himself to be a fool.

WILLIAM SHAKESPEARE, *AS YOU LIKE IT*

TALLULAH STARPOODLE, 12, Mini Poodle

VINCE, 9, Crossbreed

You can **live** to be a hundred if you *give up* all the things that make you **want** to live to be a hundred.

WOODY ALLEN

PHILLY, 13, Mixed Breed

VIVIAN, 15, Mixed Breed

ZOE, 11, Great Dane X

WALNUT, 14, Cocker Spaniel

BARNEY, 16.5, Beagle

QUINN, 8, KENDALL, 10, Boxers

# Make
## *new*
# friends.

WOOKIE, 11, Shitzu

ZAC, 11, Staffy X

ZEUS, 10, French Bulldog

ZEUS, 13, Bully Breed

# Knowing *yourself* is the beginning of all wisdom.

ARISTOTLE

TWIGGY, 8, Mixed Breed, CHOPPER, 9, Amstaff x Staffordshire Bull Terrier & BONNIE, 8, Bull Terrier

ZIGGY, 11.5, Cavalier King Charles Spaniel

ZOE, 10, Standard Schnauzer

WALLY, 8, Bearded Collie

# Dogs are better than human beings because they *know* but do not *tell*.

EMILY DICKINSON

# ACKNOWLEDGEMENTS

Many thanks to the dogs who participated in this project and to their humans that helped make it possible.

To my editor and friend Monique Butterworth for having faith in my work.

To my son Rogan for being my chauffeur on long shoot days, for running my dogs when I was away for work and for being the ultimate social media manager.

To Mom and Dad who always indulged my passion for dogs and horses. Don (Dad) never got to see the finished collection but I'm pretty sure he would have loved all those gorgeous faces.

And to my friends – thank you for being the most passionate group of animal lovers ever. You are an incredible bunch and I am very grateful to have you in my life.

Special thanks to Angela Beer who walked the aisles of the New York Book Fair with me days on end, and who has passionately been a supporter of my photography. And, to my mate Craig Dunn from Paw Justice who continually advocates for animal welfare in New Zealand. You all rock.

Finally, to Pola my first Giant Schnauzer who inspired this collection and whose passing broke my heart.

Namaste

AMBER, 12, Hunterway

PABLO, 13, Griffin

"It came to me that every time I lose a dog, they take a piece of my heart, and every new dog who comes into my life gifts me with a piece of their heart. If I live long enough, all the components of my heart will be dog, and I will become as generous and loving as they are."

Dr Cheryl Zuccaro

First published in 2017 by New Holland Publishers
London • Sydney • Auckland

This paperback edition published in 2018 by New Holland Publishers

newhollandpublishers.com

131-151 Great Titchfield Street, London, W1W 5BB, United Kingdom
1/66 Gibbes Street, Chatswood, NSW 2067, Australia
5/39 Woodside Ave, Northcote, Auckland 0627, New Zealand

A record of this book is held at the British Library and the National Library of Australia.

ISBN 9781742573205

Group Managing Director: Fiona Schultz
Publisher: Monique Butterworth
Designer: Catherine Meachen
Production Director: James Mills-Hicks
Printer: Toppan Leefung Printing Limited

10 9 8 7 6 5 4 3 2 1

Keep up with New Holland Publishers on Facebook

facebook.com/NewHollandPublishers

£9.99